Just Like YOU

Marissa Sorocco

ISBN 979-8-89043-242-1 (paperback)
ISBN 979-8-89428-737-9 (hardcover)
ISBN 979-8-89043-243-8 (digital)

Copyright © 2024 by Marissa Sorocco

All rights reserved. No part of this publication may be reproduced, distributed, or transmitted in any form or by any means, including photocopying, recording, or other electronic or mechanical methods without the prior written permission of the publisher. For permission requests, solicit the publisher via the address below.

Christian Faith Publishing
832 Park Avenue
Meadville, PA 16335
www.christianfaithpublishing.com

Printed in the United States of America

Just like you, I have two eyes
so I can see just like you.

I have a nose, so I can breathe fresh air just like you.

5

I have two ears, so I can hear sounds and words just like you.

I have two arms, so I can give and receive big hugs just like you.

I have two legs, so I can walk just like you.

I have ten fingers and ten toes just like you.

I have a mouth just like you, but I don't speak like you. I can't use words to communicate because I have no words. I'm nonverbal, and I have autism. I stand in silence.

Everyone with autism is, in fact, unique with his or her own strengths and weaknesses. So I may look like you, but I'm not like you.

This is me happy.

This is me sad.

This is me angry and not
listening to my mom.

But I have no words, and I stand in silence.
So I may look just like you, but I'm not like you.
I'm me.

I'm different.

We are all different, and that is
what makes us all special and unique.

About the Author

As a mom of two special needs kids, Madison, age thirteen, and Tyler, age eleven, I have become too familiar with the challenges that go along with raising them in a society that does not fully understand their type of disability. While they are the most precious and cherished people in *my* life, gaining acceptance for them by the community continues to be a struggle. My daughter, who is nonverbal, inspired me to write this book and talk about her journey. I am literally and figuratively her voice since she is nonverbal. Madison looks like your average child, so people get confused when they discover that she has a disability. Since many members of society have a preconceived notion regarding what a person with a disability should look like, as a mother, I want to help educate others and show them that disabilities have many different looks and facets. Even if her story can help one person understand, it would all be worth it.

Printed in the USA
CPSIA information can be obtained
at www.ICGtesting.com
CBHW041119131124
17313CB00046B/930